THE LORD'S PRAYER

*An Intensive Study of His Message
and a Short Autobiography*

Billy Anderson

WESTBOW
PRESS
A DIVISION OF THOMAS NELSON

WestBow Press books may be ordered through booksellers or by contacting:

WestBow Press
A Division of Thomas Nelson
1663 Liberty Drive
Bloomington, IN 47403
www.westbowpress.com
1-(866) 928-1240

ISBN: 978-1-4497-8662-5 (sc)
ISBN: 978-1-4497-8663-2 (e)

Library of Congress Control Number: 2013903638

Printed in the United States of America

WestBow Press rev. date: 3/5/2013

I would like to dedicate this book first to the Lord, then to all my Christian friends and to my family. May God bless these words to bring direction and blessings to the lives of many people.

Our Father in heaven,
hallowed be your name,
your kingdom come,
your will be done,
on earth as it is in heaven.
Give us today our daily bread.
Forgive us our debts,
as we also have forgiven our debtors.
And lead us not into temptation,
but deliver us from the evil one.

(Matthew 6:9-13)

TABLE OF CONTENTS

PREFACE

AFTER SEVERAL HEARTBREAKING EXPERIENCES in life, I was given a desire to do something "heart great" for God. After my life on earth is over, I want to leave behind something that will live on and bring blessings to other generations.

This intensive study of our Lord's model prayer may be a part of that heart great experience. Only time will tell if it is. I want to submit my life to our Lord, let Him do what He wishes, and live the way He wants. At any rate, the sole purpose of this writing is to bring honor and glory to our Lord.

May He bless these words in such a way that they will achieve this goal. May the Lord continue to lead our lives and teach us how to pray.

We spend a lifetime learning how to pray and trust God. We sometimes think we know how to pray and trust, only to find out that when we get in the swamps of life's trials, we become severely tested.

B. A.
Thornton, Texas

ACKNOWLEDGMENTS

I T IS VITALLY IMPORTANT to acknowledge the assistance I received in writing this book. First and foremost I want to thank God for His inspiration and guidance as I struggled to put my thoughts on paper.

I also deeply appreciate the help provided by Delores Crabb; Shannon Poldrack and her daughter Jordan; and my two granddaughters, Shelby and Shannon Anderson. These members of Victory Baptist Church assisted with the typing of the early chapter manuscripts that provided the basis for this book.

Then, at a critical time in this work, the Lord sent another member of our church, Elisabeth Miller, who proofread the material and helped to organize it and as such served as general editor of the book.

Without the assistance of these wonderful people, I might not have been able to complete this huge endeavor.

Billy Anderson, Pastor of Victory Baptist Church
Thornton, Texas

CHAPTER I

Introduction to the Lord's Prayer

OUR PRAYER LIFE REFLECTS like a mirror our relationship with God and our dependence on Him. If we have been saved by Jesus Christ, we have a Father/child relationship with God. If we have never accepted Christ as our Savior, we have no personal relationship with God. The only way to establish a personal relationship with God is to come to Him through Jesus Christ. In the gospel of John, Jesus made this very clear when He spoke the words, "I am the way and the truth and the life. No one comes to the Father except through me" (John 14:6). He also said, "I am the gate; whoever enters through me will be saved" (John 10:9). He further said, "I tell you the truth, the man who does not enter the sheep pen by the gate, but climbs in by some other way, is a thief and a robber" (John 10:1). Jesus spoke these words, and we can, without reservation, believe what He said. Jesus Christ is the only door, and He is the only way into the kingdom of God.

This relationship brings us to the matter of prayer. If we are not saved by the blood of Jesus Christ, the Son of the Living God, the only prayer we can pray is the lost sinner's prayer: "Lord, I know that I am lost and need to be saved. Please forgive me for all my sins and save my soul." The letter to the Romans says, "Everyone who calls on the name of the Lord will be saved" (Rom. 10:13).

If we trust Him, give Him our heart and life, repent of our sins, and ask Him to save us, He will not turn us away. Until we do this, we are not qualified to pray any other prayer.

Jehovah God is the only true God, and Jesus Christ, His Son, is the only Savior of our souls. There are other religions in this world, but they are all insufficient to save us for eternity. All their leaders are dead, buried, and decayed; only Jesus Christ is alive and in God's presence. This is not a boastful assertion; it is a statement of fact made because we believe the promise of God. If we trust any religion other than Christianity, we do so at our own peril.

The Bible teaches that we will reap what we sow. If we don't allow Christ to pay for our sins with His crucifixion and death on the cross, then we will have to pay for our sins ourselves. We must remember we owe a debt we cannot pay; He paid a debt He did not owe. None of us have ever experienced from someone a greater love than this.

After salvation, we can turn to the guide He has given us as to how we must pray. We are not to use vain, meaningless repetitions or pray in such a manner that we put our self-perceived righteousness on display. That is not prayer; it is mockery before God. We must come before God in a right spirit and pray to God in a right and proper way, as stated in Matthew 6:5–9.

Now let us consider the importance of the structure of the Lord's Prayer. There are seven petitions arranged into two major divisions. There are three petitions in the first division and four in the second, and they are all addressed to our Father. In this prayer we are taught how to talk with God and meet our personal requirements so we can be heard. "Our Father" must be expressed in a state of humility, realizing that God is the Father of all people who have been saved by the blood of Jesus Christ. This relationship crosses denominational lines. No church can save us; only Christ can save. There are saved people and lost people in every church. Salvation is the result of a personal relationship with "our Father" through His Son, Jesus Christ. It is important for us to get in a Bible-believing church after salvation to nurture our newly found spiritual life.

Our heavenly Father is always available to all His children, in all nations, in every corner of the world—twenty-four hours a day, seven days a week. No pastor, no earthly being, could ever meet the needs of all people in all circumstances of life. Only God can do this. He can meet all the needs of all His children, and He can do it perfectly well. He is omnipresent (present in all places at once), omniscient (knows all our needs), and omnipotent (all powerful, the almighty God). We can always trust Him; He will keep His promises.

CHAPTER 2

Our Responsibility to Keep His Name Holy

W HAT DOES IT MEAN to profane the Lord's name? What are some ways we profane His name? These are questions we will try to fully answer in this chapter.

As Christians, we have a personal responsibility to make—and keep—His name holy. This requirement is stated in both the Old and New Testaments. In the Old Testament (Ex. 20:7), the New International Version translation reads, "You shall not misuse the name of the Lord your God, for the Lord will not hold anyone guiltless who misuses His name." The King James Version of the same passage reads, "Thou shalt not take the name of the Lord thy God in vain." In the New Testament, we are reminded how demanding and protective the Lord is about how we use His name. In fact, the very first petition in this prayer requires that we make and keep His name holy: "hallowed be your name" (Matt. 6:9).

We feel the same way about how others use our name that God does about His. If someone else were to use our name in a derogatory way, with any kind of falsehood, we would immediately get offended. God demands the same respect for His name that we demand for ours.

Profanity involves a range of behaviors. Even those who don't curse might be guilty of profanity. Profanity ranges from cursing on one extreme to treating an eternal truth lightly on the other. The practice of profanity is so prevalent that we must consider the profanity that takes place both inside and outside the sanctuary.

Let us first deal with profanity that is practiced mostly outside the church. One of the most common forms of profanity is what we call cursing with God's name. Why is it wrong? It is wrong because we are accusing God of doing something He does not and will never do. We are accusing Him of dooming or damning a person. Cursing puts that person in a position of hopelessness. If a man, woman, boy, or girl becomes doomed or damned, it is because each chose to put himself or herself in that position. God had nothing to do with it; in fact, the opposite is true. He gave His only Son to die that cruel death on the cross so everyone could escape being doomed or damned for eternity. Most people who curse don't even realize the depth of devastation they are pronouncing and don't really want this kind of eternal devastation to happen to the person they are addressing.

Profanity is practiced by the person doing the addressing. Profanity happens when irresponsible words are spoken. Damnation is a terrible state of hopelessness and possibly an eternity of unbearable suffering that can never be reversed. When a person curses others like this, it is an example of unintelligent conversation and an affront to our almighty God, who would have no part in doing such a thing. God has provided a way, through His Son's death on the cross, to keep us from this horrible state of damnation. Cursing causes a negative reflection on the person who does it. I have known some people who suffered from a severe vocabulary deficiency because they used so much foul language. If profanity was removed from their vocabulary, they could lose half or better of their capacity for speech. I have known people who not only cursed other people but also cursed inanimate objects. Cursing is worse than a bad habit; it is a severe spiritual illness that requires a change of heart.

Another form of profanity involves wearing the name Christian but dealing dishonestly with other people. This dishonesty includes lying. When we represent the name of Christ, we must tell the truth about all things. There are many circumstances in life where it is very difficult to always tell the truth and follow through with honest behavior. We must remember that the Lord observes all that we do.

There are other expressions of profanity that involve treating something that is eternally sacred with disrespect or contempt or by treating its value lightly. The list includes these acts: breaking promises we have made to God; ignoring spiritual opportunities for service that God has provided for us; not listening to a call God specifically has given to us; failing to seize opportunities to promote spiritual harmony when a possibility for division exists; pretending to do God's will when we are not really serious about doing it; and allowing ourselves to become more secular instead of becoming more spiritual. This list of offenses is by no means complete, but it demonstrates the vastness of the possibilities for profanity.

Now let us switch our attention to the profanity that takes place within the sanctuary. If there ever was a place where God's name is made holy, it is in His church, yet a substantial number of our offenses take place during our time of worship. We come into a worship service with a heart that is divided between our spiritual and secular responsibilities. Sometimes our love for material things outweighs our love for spiritual matters. Sometimes we come into a service weighed down with our pride or our problems when either can cause us to profane the Lord's name. We must not allow anything to interfere with our worship relationship with God. How many times do we come into the church to worship but our minds and hearts are centered on something else? Possibly one of our greatest sins occurs when we come before an all-forgiving God pretending to worship but harboring ill feelings and bad thoughts about someone else. If we have not forgiven everyone for everything they have done to us, we have put ourselves in a position where God cannot forgive us. With an unforgiving heart, we are only "playing church." Therefore we are guilty of profanity in God's house of worship.

In almost every church, there exists a power group who comes to run the church, not to surrender to and worship the Lord. Our profanity in the sanctuary centers on a pretended relationship with God—being a true, obedient, trusting, faithful child of God—a relationship that really does not exist.

We profane His name through the medium of song in our music program. The songs we sing are a proclamation and promise to God that we love Him and want to serve Him. But we make promises to God that we have no intention of keeping or that are impossible to keep. We sing, "There's a sweet, sweet spirit in this place," when we don't contribute much toward making the spirit sweet. We sing, "Brethren, we have met to worship," when in reality we fail to worship and surrender our hearts to Him. We sing, "Take my life and let it be consecrated, Lord, to Thee," when we don't intend to do anything with our life except keep it for ourselves. We sing, "Ready for service, lowly or great," when we are very selective about the kind of service we do. And then we sing, "I surrender all," when we don't surrender all, or anything near all, to the Lord. No one of us has ever surrendered all we are or all we have to the Lord. In sum, we are guilty of profanity when we lie to the Lord through our singing in the church service.

We profane God's name through the medium of prayer. When we are called on to lead a prayer, but our mind and heart is not involved, we let our attention wander to other things. How great is God's mercy and forgiveness! Anyone who thinks we live above sin has not comprehended what sin is. All of us who have been saved by the blood of Christ are saved sinners; we are forgiven sinners, but we are still sinners. When we repent of our sins, He is always ready to forgive us. What a wonderful loving and forgiving God we serve! What a loving and forgiving Savior we have—who died in our place on that cruel cross to make this forgiveness possible!

CHAPTER 3

Seeking God's Kingdom

THE LORD'S PRAYER IS the New Testament parallel of the Ten Commandments found in Exodus 20:1–19.

The first three petitions of the Lord's Prayer ("Hallowed be Your name," "Your Kingdom come," "Your will be done") and the first four commandments of the Ten Commandments focus on a right relationship with God.

The latter four petitions of the Lord's Prayer (regarding daily bread, debts, temptation, and deliverance from evil) address our personal needs. And the latter portion of the Ten Commandments has five commandments that are ethical in nature and teach us how to relate to those around us.

The Lord's Prayer is 43 percent God centered, while the Ten Commandments are 45 percent God centered. The fifth commandment, about honoring one's father and mother, serves as a transition between the two sections of the Ten Commandments, and it addresses our responsibility to God and man. (See the chart comparing the Ten Commandments and the Lord's Prayer provided as an appendix at the end of this book.)

Together the Lord's Prayer and the Ten Commandments teach us that we must honor God in our lives first, teach us how to live together, and show us how to pray. This relationship between us, as believers, and God allows us to pray and have Him meet our personal needs.

In May 2012, Federal Judge Michael F. Urbanski of the US District Court in Roanoke, Virginia, presided over a case brought by the American Civil Liberties Union on behalf of an unnamed student against Narrows High School in Giles County, Virginia. The student, an atheist, claimed that a copy of the Ten Commandments hanging on the wall in the hallway made him feel like an outsider. The lawsuit demanded the removal of the Ten Commandments from the school hallway. The Ten Commandments were part of an exhibit of historically significant documents that included the Magna Carta, the Mayflower Compact, the Declaration of Independence, the Gettysburg Address, and many others.

After hearing this case, Judge Urbanski ordered that the first four commandments be removed. The other six could remain on the wall.

In this ruling, the judge took out the commandments that are the heart and power of the Ten Commandments. The latter six will only work after we obey the first four. The first four commandments are the ones that get us and keep us in a right relationship with God. Those who wanted God's name out of everything but couldn't get it done by popular vote were able to achieve their goal through the ruling of one appointed judge whose position makes him publicly unaccountable for his decisions.

We don't need to be taking God out of everything. We must start putting God back *into* everything.

In this study, we are talking about a kingdom coming into our hearts. We are talking about God's kingdom. Jehovah God is our King. "Thy Kingdom Come." God's kingdom can come only after we make His name holy in our lives. This is the second petition of the Lord's Prayer.

Every kingdom must have a king. The king of *this* kingdom is Jehovah God in three Persons. They are God the Father, God the Son, and God the Holy Spirit. All three have their own responsibilities.

God the Father is the Creator of the heavens and earth, which includes all planets and the universe as a whole.

Jesus Christ agreed to be the sacrificial Lamb who would pay the sin debt of all believers by dying on the cruel cross, by being buried and raised from the grave, and by ascending back to His Father. From there, He makes intercession for each and every one of us.

The Holy Spirit is the agent to convict us and make us aware of our need for God, to lead us to repent of our sins, and after we confess our desire to be saved, to come into our lives and seal our salvation. Second Corinthians says, "Now it is God who makes both us and you stand firm in Christ. He anointed us, set his seal of ownership on us, and put his Spirit in our hearts as a deposit, guaranteeing what is to come" (2 Cor. 1:21–22). In the gospel of John, Jesus says, "But the Counselor, the Holy Spirit, whom the Father will send in my name, will teach you all things and will remind you of everything I have said to you" (John 14:26).

We must give the Lord an invitation to come into our hearts. "Your kingdom come" (Matt. 6:10). There can be no limitations on our part. If He is coming as a king, we must allow Him to rule as a king. The translation of the Greek words is "Let it come the kingdom of Thee." This amounts to an open invitation with no restrictions. It also amounts to a voluntary invitation. The word "let" means we have a choice; it means we are in control of what happens in our lives. We can let it happen or not let it happen.

We can't blame others for the choices we make; we are solely responsible for those choices. There are consequences that go with every choice we make. If we make the wrong choice about our lives, we are going to pay the price. If we make the right choice, the greatest portion of the blessing will be ours, and others around us will also rejoice.

"But seek first his kingdom and his righteousness, and all these things will be given to you as well" (Matt. 6:33). This kingdom is different from all other kingdoms. Earthly kingdoms are established by coup or by succession of a king's family and are ruled by force, coercion, and threats. The kings or rulers will kill their citizens if they refuse to obey the laws of their kingdom. God, through His love, compassion, forgiveness and grace invites us into His Kingdom. This kingdom can be entered only on a voluntary basis. Through the experience of the fall in the garden of Eden, sin came into the world and caused an alienation from God that affected the entire human race. This event established a sin culture that caused all people to lose their status of innocence. Therefore, every person was born into a culture of sin and became a sinner. David acknowledged this in a psalm: "Surely I have been a sinner from birth, sinful from the time my mother conceived me" (Ps. 51:5). So the fall in the garden of Eden universally brought a sinful condition to everyone, even those who would be born into future generations. We are born into a fallen race of people without our consent. It is Satan's desire to deprive us of the privilege of consent.

God could have just left us without His kingdom and without the hope of eternal salvation. He certainly would have been justified in doing this. But this was not what He chose to do. Rather, in a pre-creation meeting with the Son and the Holy Spirit, He chose to make a way for mankind to be reinstated (see Matt.

25:34). However, there was one requirement: it had to be done on an individual basis. There would be no plan of redemption that automatically reinstated everyone regardless of whether they wanted to be reinstated. God's plan of redemption was different from Satan's plan of destruction. Satan caused everyone to be a sinner without any opportunity for choice.

God's plan was different in this respect: If He was going to send His only Son into the world to die on the cruel cross and be resurrected from the grave, only those who would love and accept His Son as their Savior would be eligible for this redemption. This means that each one of us must trust and accept His Son as our Savior individually in order to get this redemption. This is not a wholesale transaction like the fall; it involves individual choice. God prepared for us to make a personal profession of belief in Him through His Son, Jesus Christ. The death and resurrection of His Son was the only way we as individuals could be redeemed from our lost condition. "For he chose us in him before the creation of the world to be holy and blameless in his sight. In love he predestined us to be adopted as his sons through Jesus Christ, in accordance with his pleasure and will—to the praise of his glorious grace, which he has freely given us in the One he loves" (Eph. 1:4–6). He chose His Son, Christ, to be our Savior, and He chose all who are in Christ.

The letter to the Romans says,

"That if you confess with your mouth, "Jesus is Lord," and believe in your heart that God raised him from the dead, you will be saved. For it is with your heart that you believe and are justified, and it is with your mouth that you confess and are saved. As the Scripture says, "Everyone who trusts in him will never be put to shame." For there is no difference between Jew and Gentile—the same Lord is Lord of all and richly blesses all who call on him, for, "Everyone who calls on the name of the Lord will be saved." (Rom. 10:9–13)

This leaves all of us with the individual responsibility to repent of our sins, confess our sins and sinful condition to the Lord Jesus Christ, and ask Him to come into our hearts. After we surrender our hearts to Him, we are saved—we are spiritually "born again." The Bible verifies we can receive this new birth. John 3:16 says, "For God so loved the world that he gave his one and only Son, that whoever believes in him shall not perish but have eternal life." What a wonderful kingdom God offers us! There has never been another kingdom that could even begin to compare to the kingdom of God.

We have a personal responsibility to invite God to bring His kingdom into our hearts to stay. He does not want merely a part-time abode. He is not interested in coming to visit for a while and then leaving with the hope of returning later. He does not want to put His kingdom in the closet of our hearts or stay in the bedroom with the door shut while we allow unsavory visitors to come and stay awhile. God is not interested in a partial or temporary kingdom. If He brings His kingdom into our hearts, He brings it to stay.

When God moves His kingdom into our hearts, He brings all His relatives with Him. His relatives all have names. Their names are Love, Compassion, Forgiveness, Grace, Mercy, Faith, Repentance, and Prayer, among many others. None of His relatives can be left outside. They come as a group or they don't come at all. This is a highly personal experience; it can only be between each of us and God. No one else can make the decision for us or influence our choice even though they could be affected by it. This decision to accept God into our hearts is ours and ours alone.

We cannot allow our hearts to become divided. God is not willing to share the throne of His kingdom with anyone else. In Exodus, He says, "I am the Lord your God, who brought you out of Egypt, out of the land of slavery. You shall have no other gods before me" (Ex. 20:2–3). And in the gospel of Matthew, Jesus tells His disciples, "No one can serve two masters. Either he will hate the one and love the other, or he will be devoted to the one and despise the other. You cannot serve both God and Money" (Matt. 6:24). The reference to money in this verse means wealth, material things, etc., that are objects of worship. God wants our primary love and will not be satisfied with less, for we are incapable of serving God and a false god at the same time and loving both of them equally. God demands us to have an undivided heart. This is a constant struggle we face as Christians. You must strive to love the Lord our God "with all your heart and with all your soul and with all your mind. This is the first and greatest commandment" (Matt. 22:37–38). These are the words of our Lord and Savior, Jesus Christ, to every one of us. God will not agree that we can have a divided kingdom in our hearts. Satan will see to it that situations and events will come into our lives to divide our loyalty. He will use suffering, selfishness, heartache, loneliness, anger, and hatred, along with worry, which God views as distrust. The last thing Satan wants us to have is a heart that is totally ruled by Jehovah God.

God's kingdom is enduring and everlasting. When His kingdom is established in our hearts, our spiritual life is set in motion and will last forever. His is a kingdom that has no end. These earthly bodies will die and decay, but our spirits will live forever. This means that when His kingdom comes into our hearts, we are already involved in eternal life. We have eternal life in our hearts while we are on this earth, but there is another part of eternal life after this world. For everyone who has been born again, heaven is our future home. May His kingdom grow stronger in all our hearts through our trusting in God and Christ on a daily basis. Let us think about His kingdom every day to keep our spiritual lives strong. His kingdom is our hope.

CHAPTER 4

Doing God's Will

A FTER WE ARE SAVED (born again) we face some of the greatest challenges of our lives. Many of these challenges revolve around our unwillingness to let God's will rule and lead our lives. A raw translation from the Greek is "Let it come about the will of thee, as in heaven also on earth." The word "let" means we are in control. We allow certain loves or interests to come into our lives; we also determine how much ruling force they will have. This third petition in the model prayer sets as its the standard *the way God's will is being done in heaven*. Of course, the will of God will not be done perfectly here on earth because we are not perfect people. But the heavenly standard still should be our goal. Since we have obeyed the first part of this verse and have allowed the kingdom of God to come into and rule our hearts, our lives should revolve around knowing and doing the will of God.

What do we mean when we use the word "will"? It is the power behind something our mind has chosen to do. It involves the dedication and energy it takes to complete that decision. It is intentional.

We should know it is not always going to be easy to do the will of God. There will be times and circumstances that will make it hard to choose to do what we know is right. We would like for the will of God to prevail, but when God calls us to change a particular belief or lifestyle, making the right choice suddenly becomes more difficult. It is likely that most of us have already faced some of these trials multiple times. It is also likely that we have been victorious in some of these experiences and defeated in others. It all depends on how much faith we have maintained in our Lord. We can expect that trials will come, and we must have the Lord's help to emerge from our trials in victory. We must strive to keep our faith in the Lord strong. When we come into the kingdom and surrender to do His will, we will not experience a flat line of faith or faithfulness. It will be more like a roller coaster ride. We will have our challenges and our ups and downs. Every day, and sometimes every hour, we will be faced with new challenges that test our faith in our Lord. Sometimes we are obedient and do His will; but at other times we choose to do our own. When we choose our own way and will, we are always the loser.

There is a story told about a ship captain's near-catastrophic experience in the early days of our nation. He was sailing his vessel in a thick fog off the east coast of the United States, in the dead of the night. As the story goes, the ship's navigator suddenly detected a light directly in front of their vessel.

The captain of the ship was immediately alerted, and he took charge of the situation. He received a message from the other party saying, "Your ship is in danger. Turn thirteen degrees to your right."

The captain was an arrogant man, and he was infuriated by the command. He gave his name and said, "I have been a captain on the high seas for more than thirty years. I am commanding you to turn *your* vessel thirteen degrees to the left."

He then received another message, "I am a seaman first class, and I am instructing you to turn your vessel thirteen degrees to the right."

The captain was even more infuriated by the order of a seaman first class. He responded, "I am the captain of this ship, and you do not give me orders. I am commanding you to turn your vessel immediately thirteen degrees to your left."

The response came back, "I am commanding you for the last time to turn your vessel thirteen degrees to the right. You are about to crash your ship on the rocks. This is the last message you will get from this lighthouse."

Whether this story is true or not, it gives a perfect example of the damage that can be done when there is a test of wills. In this instance it involved the possible destruction of a ship and loss of some lives. But when we get into a test of wills with God, there can be eternal harm done not only to our earthly lives, but also to our souls. Spiritual surrender on our part is always the best option. We can always trust God. He is omniscient (all knowing) and always has our best interest in everything He does in our lives.

As varied as we are in our opinions, only God and His will can bring us together in unity. It requires us to surrender our will in favor of His will. Doing this becomes a blessing to the kingdom of God and to everyone who is in it. It allows us to live a better life on earth and gives us heavenly eternal rewards when this life is over. God's complete will is a reality in heaven, but it is still a work in progress in this world.

Our adversary, Satan, will be constantly trying to interfere with us doing God's will in our lives. As we individually do the will of God, others are encouraged to do the same. We all face problems in life that we just cannot solve. When we struggle to the point that we realize we cannot solve a problem on our own, we turn it over to God and ask Him to solve it. He might remove the problem entirely, or He might modify the problem and give us the strength to deal with it. But even if He does not choose to remove our problem, once He gets His hands on it, it will not look the same. He may choose not to remove a mountain that we face in our lives, but He will certainly help us climb it.

It is important that we have the patience to allow God's will to work itself out. Years ago, as a young pastor, I was struggling with a problem of disharmony in our church. There was an older lady in our church whom I greatly respected and trusted. I went by to visit her one day knowing she was concerned about the situation. I brought up the subject, and to my surprise she said, "I prayed about that problem and turned it over to the Lord and have not worried about it since." She had found the secret of how to trust God and let Him work out His will.

On that occasion, I learned a great lesson—we must take our problems to the Lord and leave them there. We must take our problems to the Lord and have the patience to allow Him to work them out. God neither keeps time like we do nor marches to our drum beat. His way is always the better way. When God solves our problems, He does not always do it the way we think it should be done; but His way is always the right way.

Years ago I knew a spiritual lady in our community who demonstrated love, understanding, and compassion. I remember her saying, "When our will prevails it can become a contradiction to the harmony of God's kingdom, and it can become a note of discord in the angelic choir." We must be careful that we don't ignore doing the will of God and thereby possibly become a negative factor in His kingdom.

When we take a problem to the Lord, He wants us to give it

to Him and trust Him to take care of it. Our only other option is to take care of it ourselves. If our spiritual eyes are open, the proper choice is very evident. God can do far more for us, and with us, than we could ever do for ourselves.

It is important for us to know the will of God for our lives, and He has made it possible for us to have this knowledge. Ephesians 1:9 says, "And he made known to us the mystery of his will according to his good pleasure, which he purposed in Christ." The Greek word *gnorisas* (translated "making known") in that verse tells us that God has gone to great efforts to make His will known to us. The word "making" shows this is an ongoing process. He not only makes an effort to show us His will but also makes continuing and successive efforts to keep showing us His will. We are not deprived of access to the knowledge of His will; it is there for us if we are willing to surrender and see. God never abandons His children—He always guides us.

In Romans 7:14–25, Paul discusses various aspects of the spiritual war in which we are engaged. He talks about the sin principle that is within us as a result of Eve and Adam's choice in the garden of Eden. He said the sin principle makes him do what he does not want to do and hinders him in fighting this spiritual war. Although Paul spoke in the first person singular, this problem was not his alone. In all Scripture the primary message is to those individuals who were involved in the actual experiences. But every passage of Scripture also has a secondary message—every scriptural message also applies to each of us. Therefore, we must attempt to do the will of God in the midst of all the spiritual warfare that surrounds us. This means we must be anchored in our faith and commitment to our Lord, Jesus Christ, if we are to succeed in doing God's will.

Many years ago, I heard a preacher give this illustration in his sermon. I don't remember the other parts of his sermon; in fact, I don't even remember the preacher's name. But I do remember the story:

> The preacher had visited a revival at a church on an American Indian reservation, and there was an Indian man in attendance they called "Chief." One night they were having a testimonial service, and Chief stood up to give his testimony. He had lived a mean and tough life until he was saved, but now he tried to honor God in all he did. In his testimony he said, "Brothers and sisters in Christ, I have two dogs fighting in my life all the time. One is a black dog, and he pulls on me to do everything that is wrong. The other is a white dog, and he tries to get me to do everything that is right." Then he sat down.
>
> Another Indian man from the other side of the auditorium arose and said, "Chief, which dog usually wins the fight?"
>
> Chief arose and said, "The dog that usually wins the fight is the one that I say *sic 'em* to."

In our spiritual warfare we have a lot to say about who wins the battle in choosing to do God's will.

In closing this chapter, I want to leave you with this poem that I think is relevant to this topic :

Answered Prayer
I asked for strength,
that I might achieve;
I was made weak,
that I might learn to obey.

I asked for health,
that I might do greater things;
I was given infirmity,
that I might do better things.

I asked for riches,
That I might be happy
I was given poverty,
That I might be wise.

I asked for power,
That I might have the praise of men;
I was given weakness,
That I might feel my need for God.

I asked for all things,
That I might enjoy life;
I was given life,
That I might enjoy all things.

I received nothing I asked for—but I received all that I had hoped for; almost despite myself, my unspoken prayers were answered. I am, among all men, most richly blessed.

—Unknown Confederate Soldier

CHAPTER 5

God Provides for Our Daily Needs

"**G**IVE US THIS DAY, our daily bread." When Jesus spoke these words, He was offering help to all of His children, regardless of our needs. The Greek word *arton* (translated "bread") has multiple meanings and can be an all-inclusive word. The root word in the Greek is *artos*, which literally means "bread" or "food." Bread was a staple in the diet of the people of that day. A deeper meaning is this: "Christ will meet your basic needs." He will provide the things we really need, not necessarily all the things we want. There is not one of us who could not live our life on a lot less than we have, and most of us have had periods in our lives where we did have a lot less than we now have.

The plural Greek word *arton* has an expanded meaning to include food for the needy. Our church does a good job in providing food for those who have fallen on hard times. In helping others, we must lead them to help themselves. We must be careful not to enable laziness or an attitude of entitlement on the part of those who need help. We are to help them as they strive to help themselves.

If we give a family fish to eat for one meal, when the fish is eaten, it is all gone. But if we feed them fish, teach them how to fish, possibly help them get a fishing pole, and teach them how to dig for bait, they can have many future meals as a result of our help. We must show responsible compassion in helping people.

We have had numerous people stop at our church, tell us they were traveling through town, and ask for money for gasoline. We have a charge account with a local merchant where we can send the travelers to get fuel. Some of these people, however, only wanted money for cigarettes, beer, wine, and liquor; so we stopped giving money. We were victims of a scam, and we did not want to get involved in enabling these people to practice their art of deception. Now we only buy them a limited amount of fuel. We might provide them with some sandwiches and drinks and if there is a small child, some baby needs. We will also consider providing them with other things they really need, but we will not give them money.

We must be responsible in our compassion and in the way we help people. At the same time, we must preserve the dignity of the people we are helping. We must invest the Lord's money wisely. We must encourage others to work and to provide for their own needs. This means families have to assume the responsibility to get a good education so they can get a good job to help themselves become self-sufficient.

Many of the problems we see in our nation today are caused by irresponsible parents who failed to teach their children personal responsibility. The Bible is very clear about how we are to help others. Jesus said in the gospel of Matthew, "The poor you will always have with you" (Matt. 26:11). Helping the needy is a wonderful opportunity for churches to minister, but we must minister responsibly.

Paul warned about the negative results of idleness. In writing to the Thessalonians, Paul reminds them that he worked as a tent maker and did not live off the people (see 2 Thess. 3:6–10). Paul says, "If a man will not work, he shall not eat" (2 Thess. 3:10). In the Old Testament, Exodus says, "Remember the Sabbath day by keeping it holy. Six days you shall labor and do all your work …" (Ex. 20:8–9). This is a command not only to keep our day of worship holy but also to work.

Work has always been a part of God's plan. He gives us the health and opportunity to work, thereby meeting our need for daily bread. Work is not a part of the curse resulting from the fall of mankind in the garden of Eden. Work—to dress the garden and keep it—was a part of Adam and Eve's responsibility. It is our responsibility to work in order to fulfill daily needs for ourselves and our family. Work is good for us, and it has always been a part of God's plan to meet our daily needs.

Perhaps we have made a mistake with our children by not teaching them the value of work and requiring them to work. Many of us who have had a hard life have wanted our children to have a better and easier time than we had. However good our intentions were, we may have done our children a disservice by making life too easy for them. Hard work and hard times taught us responsibility and discipline and made us better people in the process.

We should help those who truly cannot take care of themselves. We must not do everything for them and strip them of their dignity, even though our intentions are good. No one can be as proud of or appreciative of something that is free as one can be about something that was earned. This is the tragic mistake our government has made in its so-called welfare programs. Many groups and families have been relegated to a life of poverty because they have been stripped of the desire to work and achieve. Every one of us does better, both financially and in growth and maturity as a person, when we work for what we get.

Socialistic types of governments have never thrived and progressed. These governments have never improved the lives of their people. Their citizens usually lose their challenge for personal achievement. But we do not need to depend upon someone else for what we can do for ourselves.

As Christians, we must be willing and available to provide aid for those who honestly need assistance. However, our help should be withdrawn from them as soon as possible so that we can help someone else who has a legitimate need. This enables us to avoid destroying their spirit of self-sufficiency and self-respect. We must allocate God's resources wisely so they can be used to assist the maximum number of people.

Jesus said, "Give us this day, our daily bread." Let's take this statement apart so we can understand the full meaning of His words.

God is the source of all giving. Not only must we go to Him, asking Him to meet our daily needs, but also we must give Him all the credit and glory when He responds to our prayer request. Asking God to meet our daily needs should be a daily occurrence. Some days our problems may seem more serious than others, but the grace and sufficiency of the Lord is always there to meet every need of our lives. God can meet all our needs without any difficulty. We recognize (acknowledge) that the daily bread is what is given and that almighty God is the giver. Remember the location of this petition; it is the first one listed in the second division or grouping of concepts.

The Greek word *arton* (bread) is a noun in the accusative case, and it is the direct object of the verb *give*. Since the giving must be done by the giver (God), this means that almighty God is in control. God is the giver, and we are the ones who are in need of His giving. Before we can receive His gifts, we must honor His name, be a member of His kingdom, and always be striving to do His will. After we do these things, we are in a position to pray that God will meet our daily needs. How can we expect a gift if we don't honor the giver?

In the Old Testament, a proverb provides, "Two things I ask of you, O Lord; do not refuse me before I die: ... give me neither poverty nor riches, but give me only my daily bread" (Prov. 30:7–8). When we honor God and depend on His leadership in our lives, we will strike a reasonable and happy medium in the way that we live. We need to plan and prepare for the future, but not at the expense of neglecting the future of our souls. This principle was true and needed in Old Testament times just like it is true and needed today.

Now we are ready to pray for our personal needs. How can we ask the giver to give, if we have failed to honor the giver? Until Christ is our Savior, and God is our Father, we are not qualified to pray for God to meet our daily needs. But when we make Him Lord, He stands ready to supply all our needs. When we trust God for all provisions of life and obey His word and will, He will put more food on our table than we can eat. We don't love and trust Him in order to get what we need; we love Him because it is the right thing to do. His blessings in our lives are a natural result of our obedience. He is God, and we are mankind, and we must never forget that pecking order. God is always ready to protect His children.

We must pray in accordance with God's will. We who are ignorant of our own needs beg often for things that will bring us harm. Our wise God protects us by denying what we ask. He does this for our own good, and we profit by His denial.

He does not complain about the difficulty of the problems, as do some of His children. Our most difficult problems are solved on a routine basis by our Lord, with grace to spare.

It would help us if problems called in advance and made an appointment, but this is not the way it happens. It would be better for us if problems came one at a time, but Satan does not work this way. Problems usually come in clusters in the Enemy's attempt to overwhelm us. Satan wants to swamp us with problems in order to neutralize or destroy our faith in God and make us defeated Christians.

"Give us": This is our request for God to help us. Satan wants to make this a personal battle between him and us. He wants God and Christ kept out of it. We need to pray for God to stay in the battle and fight it for us. But if Satan can succeed in making us feel discouraged and defeated to the point we lose our trust in God, he has us right where he wants us. He will have us in a one-on-one battle with him. That is the way he wants it, and we will lose that battle with him every time. Our only hope is to keep our faith in God strong and allow Him to fight our spiritual battles and provide for our daily needs.

This is a prayer request to almighty God to help us overcome anything Satan throws our way in addition to meeting our other daily needs. The Greek word *hemon* is translated "of us." This is our bread; the box of supplies has our name on it.

"This day": When Jesus specifies these words for us to pray, He is talking about His daily availability. Today, tomorrow, and every day, God is always present, available, and ready to meet all of our needs—no matter how many there are, no matter how big and difficult they may be, and no matter how many times they are repeated or how fast they come. Our God is always ready and able to meet every need we have every day.

"Our daily bread": Luke 11:3 puts a little different slant on the subject of providing bread. He says in this passage, "Give us each day our daily bread." The words transliterated from the Greek read, "The bread of us—belonging to the morrow give us each day."

Matthew uses the Greek word translated "daily" to mean that specific day, but Luke uses that word in a more general sense to include tomorrow's bread. This does not mean one is right and the other is wrong. I really see no conflict between the two statements. We serve a great God who can and will provide for our daily needs today, tomorrow, next week, and every day that follows. This expanded thought just reveals more of the greatness of our God. Our problem does not lie in God's inability to meet our needs; our problem lies in our unwillingness to trust God in all circumstances of life. Some of our days are going to have more trials in them than others; therefore, it is important to trust Him all day, every day. He will certainly do His part in taking care of His children.

To close this chapter, here are several lessons for life we should learn from this prayer:

1. *The words of this prayer are not a license for laziness.*

2. *Work is very important, and it has always been a part of God's plan. Before the fall in the garden of Eden, Adam and Eve were given the responsibility to dress and keep the garden. In Exodus 20:8–9 we are commanded to work six days a week.*

3. *When giving assistance to others, we must preserve the dignity of those who are helped.*

4. *We must teach personal responsibility. We have moved in the direction of a socialist, entitlement nation, and if this is not reversed, it will destroy America. Look at what it has done to the European nations.*

All of these are lessons we should learn, but there is one more lesson we must learn: we, as Americans, must repent of our sins and come back to God. We have an excellent guide if we follow the teachings of the Lord's Prayer.

We spend a lifetime learning how to pray and trust God. We must not become so weary and discouraged that we lose our spiritual tenacity.

Squirrel and Bunny

By Billy Anderson

Squirrel said to Bunny,
"We must trust God for our needs.
He lovingly provides us with
Green sprouts and nuts and seeds."

Bunny said to Squirrel,
"If man would trust Him, too,
God would daily care for his needs
Like He does for me and you."

CHAPTER 6

God Requires Total Forgiveness

I N THIS CHAPTER, WE will make an in-depth study of the second petition in the second section of the Lord's Prayer: "Forgive us our debts, as we also have forgiven our debtors" (Matthew 6:12). In the Greek text, the word for "have forgiven" is *aphekamen*, and it is in the past tense, meaning it has already been done. That one Greek word unlocks all the other doors of forgiveness and makes our forgiveness from God possible. But on the other hand, it can also lock all the doors of forgiveness if we refuse to forgive. Until we forgive all others for everything, we put ourselves in a position where we cannot be forgiven for anything.

Notice how important forgiveness is with our Lord. It is second only to receiving the bread of life. God has made us in such a manner that we need bread. As a member of the human race, each of us needs forgiveness. God wants to feed and care for His children, and He wants to forgive us for all our sins and transgressions. After examining what sin is, we should all have a greater awareness of how sinful we are.

The five Greek words we will study that are translated "sin" are not the only Greek or Hebrew words translated "sin" in the Bible. However, they are the most predominantly used words to explain the kinds of sins. Other Greek words are used, but these five words will cover the vast majority of references to sin in the New Testament.

In this study, we must remember that the fall of mankind and the corresponding spiritual death came before the Mosaic Law. So our sins are against God first and then against the law God gave to Moses on Mount Sinai. Every person who has been born since Adam and Eve has been born into a fallen race—Jews and Gentiles alike. This subject is addressed in Romans: "Therefore, just as sin entered the world through one man, and death through sin, and in this way death came to all men, because all sinned—for before the law was given, sin was in the world. But sin is not taken into account when there is no law" (Rom. 5:12–13). Death reigned and affected all of humanity from Adam to the time of Moses. After the fall in the garden of Eden, sin multiplied and affected every generation of people. God sent a flood to harness man's sinful behavior, but it only spread and got worse. In our world today, most people have turned against God and Christ. Satan has blinded the minds of people to the extent that many people want God and Christ out of our government, our schools, our recreational activities, and even our patriotic events. This shows us that sin is not just an ancient problem; it is a present problem and will also continue to be a future problem.

The eternal, everlasting truth is that Jehovah God is our Creator, and Jesus Christ is the only Savior for our souls. We must bring them back into every aspect of our lives and repent of our sins. As this study shows, we need forgiveness from God, but we must forgive all others before we can be forgiven.

We will extensively consider three out of the five Greek words usually translated "sin" and their meanings as used in the accounts of the Lord's Prayer in Matthew 6:12, 14–15 and Luke 11:4.

The first and most widely used word for sin is *hamartia* (ham-ar-tee'-uh). This describes our condition of falling short of the righteousness of God. Romans 3:10 says, "As it is written: "There is no one righteous, not even one." Then in Romans 3:23, the Bible says, "for all have sinned and fall short of the glory of God." Further evidence of our sinful condition is recorded in I John 1:8: "If we claim to be without sin, we deceive ourselves and the truth is not in us." Also, David said in the Fifty-first Psalm, "Surely I have been a sinner from birth, sinful from the time my mother conceived me" (Ps. 51:5). Luke uses the word *hamartia* in Luke 11:4 in his account of the Lord's Prayer. These scriptural accounts establish the fact that we are alienated from God by our sin and need to be forgiven and saved by our Savior.

Hamartia shows we were born in sin; we were born into a sinful culture, and we are automatically sinners. God is a gracious and merciful God. He provides safety for babies until they reach the age of accountability, which can range from seven up to twelve years old, depending on the development of the child and how much he or she is exposed to the salvation message. Children become responsible for their souls and spiritual lives when they know and understand right from wrong. Individuals who are mentally challenged may never become accountable for their sins. Both groups are safe in the arms of Jesus. There is no risk for them because they are protected and kept in our Savior's arms. These scriptures verify that all of us are born in sin, and we must either be safe or saved by the blood of Jesus Christ and His sacrifice on the cross to pay our sin debt for us.

The word *hamartia* evolved from an archer's experience. This archer would practice shooting his arrows at a target he had set up. In his practice, all of his arrows were falling short of the target; even his best shots were falling short. Thus *hamartia* was born, and it means this: "all of us fall short of the righteousness of God." Even with our best efforts we cannot hit the target of God's righteousness. This form of sin includes everyone—the best people in the community, the worst people in the community, those who work in civic affairs to make their community better, and those who don't care about their community or country. This type of sin came about with that fatal decision made by Adam and Eve in the garden of Eden. They created a massive debt resulting in the fall of all mankind. Everyone from that time on became a sinner and lost their innocence. We are sinners by birth, we are lost, and we have no hope without Christ as our Savior. We must all be saved through placing our personal faith in Jesus Christ.

The second Greek word in the sin family is *paraptoma* (par-ap'-to-mah) and is translated as follows: "a false step; a blunder." It refers to someone who unintentionally steps across a forbidden line. We did not intend to do it but were pulled across the line by circumstances or other people—we still, however, transgressed and sinned against God. This is called a trespass against God caused by careless or reckless living. The word *paraptoma* can also be correctly translated as this: "a trespass; a deviation from uprightness and truth." Under either translation it is an act that is against the righteous standard required by our Lord. The fact that it was unintentional does not remove the responsibility for the act. We must realize that we all commit unintentional sins in our life. Sins of *omission* fall into this category. Many arrogant and spiritually defiant people who refuse to acknowledge this sin will be humbled in the Day of Judgment, but it will be too late for repentance then. They think it is not a big deal now, but they will realize their mistake in that day.

The third word used to represent sin is *parabasis* (par-ab'-as-is). It means this: "the act of excessive and enormous transgression of a stated law or a given commandment." This sin occurs when we intentionally choose to step across a forbidden line and trespass against the righteousness and will of God. This is planned and chosen sin; sins of *commission* fall into this category.

The fourth word used to represent sin is *anomia* (an-om-ee'-ah), which is the total disregard for and defiance of God's righteous nature and all of God's laws. We have many people today who want God out of everything. This is spiritual lawlessness. Many people deny the existence of God, and an even greater number do not believe Jesus Christ is the Son of God and only Savior of mankind. Someone once said, "There are no atheists in hell." They will learn the truth, but it will be too late.

All of these sins create the fifth word, *opheilema* (of-i´-lay-mah), which means sin as a "debt" because it demands compensation and thus payment by way of punishment. It results in a void and empty relationship with God. A debt is created against God that is too great for any of us to pay. God had to send His Son into the world to die a horrible death on the cross to pay that debt for us. God foresaw this event happening before the creation of the world, and He made a way for our deliverance in the pre-creation council. *Opheilema* describes the trail of devastation that is left behind after sin does its destructive work. It is like looking at the devastation of an F5 tornado after it destroys a town.

In review, here are the names and meanings of the most prevalent sins used in the New Testament:

1. *Hamartia: falling short of the righteousness of God;*

2. *Paraptoma: unintentionally slipping across the line between right and wrong; careless and reckless living;*

3. *Parabasis: intentionally stepping across the line that is drawn between right and wrong; enjoying sin with an intent to continue practicing sin;*

4. *Anomia: lawlessness—a disregarding of all God's laws; and*

5. *Opheilema: something owed; an obligation; a description of sin's destructive damage.*

We have a tendency to categorize sin into segments that are bad and not so bad. All sin is bad, and all sin is serious. The results of sin are spiritually the same, even though the social consequences might not be the same. Our sins leave us with a debt. That debt must be rectified and paid in full. There can be no down payment or partial payment. The fact is that without Christ and His salvation, we face a debt that we can never afford to pay. We have been left with an obligation that is far beyond our ability to erase. To make it worse, there is a deadline for the payment of that debt. It has to be paid while we are still alive and have the right mental and spiritual faculties to make a total surrender of our heart and life to Jesus Christ. He is here, ready and willing to deliver us from the eternal destruction of our soul. All we have to do is trust Him and we can be saved for eternity.

Before we were saved—born again by the Holy Spirit of God—we were working for wages; but because we were working for the wrong one, our wages were death. After we were awakened and understood what was going on in our life, we changed our commitment and started serving the One whose benefits are much greater, and His reward is eternal life. This change was the most positive decision we could make in our life. Salvation is given to us by the grace of God, and the only thing required from us is a surrender of our love and allegiance to Christ. We must repent of our sins and ask Him to come into our lives and save our souls. After this we are to walk with Him, love Him, worship Him, serve Him, and trust Him with our souls for the rest of eternity. The letter to the Ephesians says, "For it is by grace you have been saved, through faith—and this not from yourselves, it is the gift of God—not by works, so that no one can boast" (Eph. 2:8–9).

Our sin debt is paid in full by Jesus Christ only, and nothing that we have done for ourselves could add anything to His grace.

We can block our own forgiveness, however, by refusing to forgive others who have offended us. We may have hard feelings toward others, even though we are partly responsible for the situation. We make critical judgments toward others that are exaggerated. We have a general dislike for certain people although there is no real basis for it. This leaves us with a spiritual condition that is not right with God, and we need a heart-cleansing experience. The only way to get this heart-cleansing experience is to ask God to forgive us for our sins. We must go to God in a state of repentance and ask Him to cleanse us from our sins and forgive us our debts. When we do this, He wipes away all our sins. But He cannot forgive us until we forgive all others for their transgressions against us.

When I was in elementary school, we had big blackboards on the front and side walls of our classroom. The teacher would use white chalk and write on those blackboards until they were full. She had a bucket of water and a big rag for cleaning. Some of us boys who often got into trouble caused her to make a deal with us. She said that if we would be good, she would let us wash the boards at the end of each period. We loved to do that, and we would leave each board wiped completely clean. This same thing happens to our hearts when we ask God to forgive our sins. He cleanses our hearts even cleaner than we cleaned those boards for our teacher.

Instead of having a dirty heart, we now have a clean heart. It is amazing how much a clean heart can change our attitudes. The people we didn't like are suddenly more likeable, and the people we resented are more acceptable. Our feelings of animosity become tempered with love and acceptance. What caused this change? We forgave others and God forgave us, which allowed this change in our lives. When we really forgive others, we must "let it go." We can't pretend to forgive and still hang on to any degree of hatred or resentment. Satan will try to revive the feelings of hatred, but we must not allow that to happen. We must forgive and let it go. If we don't, we will only add on to that sin and bring more hurt into our own lives. Over the years, I have known of people who carried a hatred for others and just would not let it die. Some had hated for so long and so intensely that the clenching of their jaws had caused their teeth to grind together and wear down to the gums. They paid a terrible physical price for their hate, but the spiritual damage done to their life was immeasurable.

This story was told in the *Evangelical Beacon* (March 15, 1980) of two families who had a bitter dispute about the property boundary on a fence line. The dispute grew more and more bitter over the years; the two families literally hated each other. The years went by and one of the elderly men became critically ill. When his life was coming to an end, he called all his sons to his hospital room. He reminded his boys of the hate that existed with the other family. Then he told his oldest son, "I am about to meet my Maker, and I have to get things squared up with the Lord. I can't afford to hate any longer, so I want you to take my place and carry on the hate for our family." What a terrible thing to wish upon his son!

There are at least two good reasons why we must be willing to forgive others for all debts or offenses committed against us: (a) we cannot get forgiveness from God for any offense we commit against Him or debts we owe Him until we have first forgiven others for all offenses they have committed against us; and (b) we cannot truly make peace with a person until we have forgiven him or her for every offense.

One of the proverbs says, "An offended brother is more unyielding than a fortified city, and disputes are like the barred gates of a citadel" (Prov. 18:19). Without forgiveness, it will not be possible to make peace with another. We know it is not always easy to forgive, but forgiving is necessary for our own spiritual and mental well-being. I once heard someone say, "Iron is consumed by its own rust." An iron pipe, if left unattended, will develop rust holes and eventually waste away. That is similar to what happens to our hearts and lives if we refuse to forgive others for everything. There can be no reservations; there can be no restrictions; there can be no exceptions. Total unconditional forgiveness is required. Anything short of total forgiveness is no forgiveness at all.

Forgiving others is not the only thing necessary for our spiritual and mental health; we must also be forgiven for our own sins, whatever type they may be. We have sins of omission in our lives—where we fail to say or do something that we should have said or done. We are expected to do something good for another just because it is the right thing to do—not because we seek some kind of payment or reward. We sometimes intend to do those good things but just don't get around to doing them. There is no telling how many opportunities to help someone we have every day but do not act upon. We may not count these sins of omission as failures, but God does. Our sins of commission are those sins we do on purpose that we should not have done. Both of these types of sins must be forgiven.

Jesus said, "Love the Lord your God with all your heart and with all your soul and with all your mind and with all your strength. … Love your neighbor as yourself. There is no commandment greater than these" (Mark 12:30–31). Whether it is on this earth, or in our next life in heaven, love is always the best way. Let us always be willing to forgive all others for everything. We will be happier and more blessed people when we do this.

CHAPTER 7

The Purpose and Meaning of Trials and Temptations

THERE IS A BIG difference between the meanings of the words *trials* and *temptations*. We will examine both words but will first consider trials in detail. Trials are good for us. Trials have a positive goal and purpose in our lives: they make us grow spiritually, become stronger in our faith, and trust in the Lord. God allows trials and testing to come into our lives; it is the method He uses to raise His children. Trials can have a positive or negative effect on our spiritual lives. The effects are positive when we walk with the Lord and trust His sustaining power. It is God's will that we allow Him to make us victorious through every trial and become a stronger Christian. However, the trials can become negative if we waver in our faith, fail to trust in our Lord, or are defeated in our struggle with Satan. It is always God's will for His children to become victorious and grow in grace, trust, love, and forgiveness.

In one major Greek-English lexicon (Bauer 1952), the base Greek word for trials is *peirasmon* (pi-ras-mon´), which is in the future tense. This means that for all of us there is always a future possibility of being confronted with trials. These trials give us the opportunity to prove ourselves by remaining faithful to our Lord. This word in Greek is in itself neutral. This indicates that trials are neither good nor bad but can become either depending on how we handle the experience and what choices we make.

James' letter to the twelve tribes which were scattered among the nations reads, "Consider it pure joy, my brothers, whenever you face trials of many kinds, because you know that the testing of your faith develops perseverance. Perseverance must finish its work so that you may be mature and complete, not lacking anything" (James 1:2–4). We must expect many kinds of trials to come into our lives. It is through these trials that God strengthens His children. It is His intention that we will be made stronger in our faith with every trial. James 1:12 reaffirms the positive result when we are victorious in our period of testing: "Blessed is the man who perseveres under trial, because when he has stood the test, he will receive the crown of life that God has promised to those who love him."

The stronger and more mature we become as Christians, the greater the demand for more severe trials. The severity of our trials must exceed our level of spiritual maturity in order for the trials to be effective in adding spiritual strength and growth to our lives. The minor trials we experience as a babe in Christ are not of sufficient intensity to make a mature Christian stronger. The Greek word *hupomone* (hoop-om-on-ay´) means this: "cheerful or hopeful endurance; patience." At the conclusion of each trial experience, we should be stronger in our faith.

From my personal experience I have learned a trial can sometimes have a negative outcome in our lives. The possibility of failure always exists. For instance,

- when faced with a trial, we must make a choice; and even when we choose to follow the positive road, we sometimes encounter problems that negate our positive choice;
- there is a possibility that positive trials may turn into negative temptations when severely enticed;
- if we become discouraged, then we may develop a position in life whereby we oppose or even hate God and the Gospel of Christ.

There are many trials that are presented to us in our Christian lives, and we must choose to walk and trust in the Lord in every circumstance. We must always remember that everything we do should be done for the honor and glory of our Lord and Savior, Jesus Christ.

Let us now consider the perils of temptation. The word *peirasmon* (translated "temptation") is used in Matthew 6:13 in the phrase "and lead us not into temptation." But there is another word in this passage that deserves our attention. The little word in the Greek, *eis* (ice), which is translated "into," has a connotation of going "into" a narrow back alley, the end of which is blocked, leaving us trapped with no way out. God would never place His children in a position like that. God does not cause His children to be tempted with sin; that is the work of Satan. If we find ourselves trapped in such a situation, God will always provide us a way of escape. However, God will not lead us out of this situation unless we want to get out of it. And once we escape, it is our responsibility not to get into that same kind of predicament again. There will be plenty of other temptations to take its place, so we must stay on guard and walk with the Lord. When a temptation arises, we can head it off by refusing to give the situation inward consideration or acceptance in our minds or hearts. We must head it off at the pass and stop it before it gets started.

Temptations are not the same for everyone, and temptations do not affect everyone the same. Since we don't all have identical weaknesses, what is a severe temptation to sin for one person may not be a temptation at all for another. One person is unmoved while another is severely tested. All temptations are dangerous and should be avoided at all costs. We must always remember that Satan is the tempter and is working hard to destroy every home, life, and soul he can. He has no future except to suffer in the fiery flames of hell for the rest of eternity. He is working hard to share his misery with every person he can.

John MacArthur addresses the close relationship between trials and temptations in his commentary on Matthew's gospel (MacArthur 1985, 395), where he says, "The root meaning has to do with a testing or proving, and from that meaning are derived the related meanings of trial and temptation. Here it seems to parallel the term evil, indicating that it has in view enticement to sin." It would be a violation of God's holiness to lead or bring any of His children into a situation that would entice us to sin. So why should we pray for God not do something that He would never do anyway? Many Bible scholars seem to think this prayer is dealing with a desire of the heart, which is the breeding ground for the conception of sin. Our goal should be to develop such a strong trust in the Lord that our faith would kill sinful desires in their infancy.

Shortly after Jesus was baptized, He was severely tempted by Satan three times. The full purpose of these temptations was to destroy His holy nature and obstruct His mission to be the Savior of all mankind. If Satan would tempt our Lord, how can we expect him to do less to us? Satan was persistent in his temptations of Jesus, and we can't expect him to be less merciless when he tempts us.

Then Jesus was led by the Spirit into the desert to be tempted by the devil. After fasting forty days and forty nights, he was hungry. The tempter came to him and said, "If you are the Son of God, tell these stones to become bread." Jesus answered, "It is written: 'Man does not live on bread alone, but on every word that comes from the mouth of God.'" Then the devil took him to the holy city and had him stand on the highest point of the temple. "If you are the Son of God," he said, "throw yourself down. For it is written: 'He will command his angels concerning you, and they will lift you up in their hands, so that you will not strike your foot against a stone.'" Jesus answered him, "It is also written: 'Do not put the Lord your God to the test.'" Again, the devil took him to a very high mountain and showed Him all the kingdoms of the world and their splendor. "All this I will give you," he said, "if you will bow down and worship me." (Matt. 4:1–9)

Notice Satan's appeal to Christ in these three instances. They were all directed at points where he felt Christ would be the weakest. Jesus had not eaten for forty days and forty nights, and

His physical body had to be terribly hungry. The stones Satan showed Christ were probably in an oval shape, looking like a loaf of bread in that day. This visual perception would only increase His feelings of hunger. Satan always knows our weakest areas and even our weakest point within those weak areas. That is where his major attack will come.

In the second temptation, he referred to power and wealth in the world and said he would give all of those things to Jesus. Satan will always promise to give things that he has no power to give or would not give even if he could. If he will lie to our Lord, he will certainty lie to us.

In the third instance, the temptation was based on human greed and desire for personal safety. But notice how he knew and used the Scripture to strengthen his argument. Satan will use any lie or trick to deceive his victims.

Notice that Satan wasted no time after Jesus was baptized by John in the Jordan River to tempt Jesus to sin. Some Bible students say these were not really temptations. That is not true; Satan was desperately trying to get the Lord to sin by obeying him. If there was not a possibility that Jesus could sin, these efforts would not be a temptation. "For we do not have a high priest who is unable to sympathize with our weaknesses, but we have one who has been tempted in every way, just as we are—yet was without sin" (Heb. 4:15). For this Scripture to be true there had to be a possibility of sin. These were occasions where the outcome was uncertain and the possibility of sinning was real. The emphasis here is not on the belief that Jesus could not sin but on the fact that He did not sin. Satan has set his aim on each of us, and he will be relentless in his efforts to get us to sin through temptation.

Peirasmos (pi-ras-mos´) is a neutral word meaning this: "a putting to proof (by experiment [of good], experience [of evil], solicitation, discipline or provocation)" (Strong 2010). We, with our level of devotion to God, make the experience turn out good or bad. With every trial or temptation, the experience can be either a great victory or a disaster—it all depends on what we do with it. The book of James describes this:

Blessed is the man who perseveres under trial, because when he has stood the test, he will receive the crown of life that God has promised to those who love Him. (James 1:12)

That is the great victory.

When tempted, no one should say, "God is tempting me." For God cannot be tempted by evil, nor does he tempt anyone; but each one is tempted when, by his own evil desire, he is dragged away and enticed. Then, after desire has conceived, it gives birth to sin; and sin, when it is full-grown, gives birth to death. (James 1:13–15)

That is the disaster.

Let us further consider the part of this passage that deals with temptations: verses 14 and 15. Now we are talking about real, destructive, and deadly temptation, whose author and driver is Satan. None of these efforts are for building and strengthening; the total aim is to damage and destroy.

James gave only one example of temptation, but we have

many weaknesses where Satan can attack us with his determined, vicious fury. Here are some areas in our lives in which we can be tempted: vanity, arrogance, power and control, sex, material greed (for money and other possessions), addiction to alcohol and drugs, fame and personal glory, gluttony (for food), ambitiousness, jealousy, covetousness, envy, cheating, loneliness, and dishonesty. All of us have areas of weakness in our lives, and Satan has made it his business to know every one of them. He also knows when we are the weakest in all of our areas of weakness. He is always ready to attack us in those areas and do as much damage as he can to our lives and futures. Countless numbers of people have had their homes and families destroyed, lost their jobs, lost the respect of people who love them, and ruined their futures by succumbing to temptations. In the midst of all this bad news, there is some good news: if we trust God and depend on Him, He will not allow more to come on us than we can bear, and He will provide us with our needed deliverance. In the ninety-first Psalm, we have His promise: "He who dwells in the shelter of the Most High will rest in the shadow of the Almighty. I will say of the Lord, "He is my refuge and my fortress, my God, in whom I trust." Surely he will save you from the fowler's snare and from the deadly pestilence" (Ps. 91:1–3). God watches out for the safety of His children.

The model prayer—the Lord's Prayer—addresses our past sins, the condition that sin left behind (*opheilema*), and the future possibility of sinning through temptations. It was necessary that we distinguish trials from temptations because their intentions are totally different. One is to strengthen our faith in the Lord; the other is to destroy and ruin our lives. Somewhere in the process of making steel, the elements must be exposed to the fire. Exposure to the fire gives strength to the steel and makes it tremendously strong.

At different points in our lives, God must subject us to the fire of trials to make us spiritually strong.

After a diamond is mined, it must be put through a cutting and grinding process. It is the cutting and grinding that brings forth the beauty and worth of the diamond. Likewise, God must allow us to go through the grinding and cutting process to bring out the beauty of our lives. After we go through these hardships and trials successfully, we are better people—with more love and compassion in our hearts than we had before.

The Lord's Prayer is not a medal of honor to be hung around the neck of victorious Christians who are battle-proven heroes of faith. Rather, it is a message of hope and strength to every believer who is involved in a daily struggle to remain faithful in their walk with the Lord. When Jesus spoke these words, He was not speaking to a group of victorious disciples who had achieved success and who had overcome the powers of Satan. Many in this group, in fact, would desert Him later when He went to the cross to die for their sins. They were expecting a messiah who would come to earth, defeat the cruel Romans, liberate them, set up an earthly kingdom, and give them positions in the government. Most of His followers were not interested in someone who came to die on a cross; they were interested in power and personal gain. As a result, many of them turned against Jesus and walked with Him no more.

We know it is not sin to be tried or tempted. When do trials or temptations become sin? It is only when we yield to a trial or temptation that it becomes sin.

While we still have life and opportunity, we must walk closely with our Lord. We will continue having battles with Satan on this earth, but we have the promise of glory and spiritual splendor waiting for us in heaven. This is the reason we must love and trust our Savior, Jesus Christ. What a future we have with our Lord!

CHAPTER 8

Being Rescued from Evil

"**B**UT DELIVER US FROM the evil one" (Matt. 6:13). We need to remember that many Bible scholars don't divide temptation and evil. They treat both of these subjects as one. There is no question about them being interrelated, but we, in this study, are treating them as two different subjects. In this chapter, we will discuss the full meaning of evil as it affects our lives in so many ways. Evil can be divided into natural evil and moral evil.

We will begin by defining natural evil and the devastating effects it can have on our lives. What is natural evil? It is the consequence of moral evil. Natural evil can be expressed in so many ways, including tornados, hurricanes, earthquakes, floods, tsunamis, wars, physical attacks, wrecks, airplane and automotive accidents, explosions, cyber-attacks, terrorism, illicit drug use, suicides, and other forms of tragedies and disasters. Natural evil expresses itself in physical damage, sickness, and death. Why is this subject included in the model of the Lord's Prayer? It is included because of the hurt and devastation natural evil can bring into the lives of so many people. It often reminds us of our need to pray.

Most property insurance policies refer to natural occurrences as "acts of God." This is not a fair accusation, because God does not make a habit of destroying anything. He may allow Satan to do it, because destruction is part of the Devil's work. But God will bring good out of it if people will allow that to happen. When individuals and nations turn against God, all He has to do is withdraw His protection and the individual or nation will self-destruct. This is what is happening in our world today. America is traveling down the same road that is destroying Europe. Bad leadership in both Europe and America has brought us to our present crisis. If Americans do not repent of our sins and come back to God, one of the greatest nations on earth will be destroyed. Think of the devastating effect this will have on individuals, families, and our once-great nation. We are facing a deadline; the time bomb is ticking, and the hour is urgent for us to turn our lives and nation around. The ball is in our court, and the great question is this: will we allow God to save our country? The principles taught in the Lord's Prayer will turn us around—but only if we obey its message.

God destroyed Sodom and Gomorrah because of their sins and iniquities. Surely America is approaching, and has possibly surpassed, their sin culture. The question is this: when is God going to back out of America, drop His protective hand, and allow us to be destroyed? Natural evil has, in the annals of time, been used to destroy elements of civilization. But God cannot be blamed for causing the destruction. Think back to the garden of Eden where Adam and Eve lived in a state of innocence. There was no moral evil. It was only after sin came in the garden and destroyed innocence that there was any moral evil.

We have discussed the dangerous effects of natural evil, but now let us consider the definition of natural evil. In *Baker's Dictionary of Theology*, we are told, "According to the Bible, natural evil is the consequence of moral evil. At first, while still sinless, man is placed in an idyllic garden, where he lives in a happy relationship with his Creator, his wife and his animals ... The day that he disobeys God, (i.e., commits moral evil), he is covered with shame, confusion and anxiety, is condemned by God and ejected from the Garden." This is a prevalent view throughout the Old Testament. Job, when hit by many forms of natural evil, came to the conclusion he was not sinless. But at times, mankind lost sight of the sinful cause for the occurrence of natural evil. Natural evil can bring harm and suffering to our bodies and lives, but it cannot damage or destroy the soul of God's faithful.

This attitude involving sin and suffering is continued in the New Testament. When we sin and turn away from God, we will suffer the result in some way. When we personally repent of our sins, we are forgiven of the sin, and judgment is removed, but most of the time, we have to live with the consequences of our sin. We may endure natural evil—suffering for years, or even a lifetime, as a consequence of the sins we commit. So it is apparent that sin and suffering are interrelated. When God chose to allow mankind the freedom of choice (free will), He knew that many would make the wrong choice, and He made provision through His Son, Jesus Christ, to offer them a way of restoration. God is not the author of sin, but He does permit sin. Through God's judgment on sin, His unlimited power is revealed. Because God loves us, forgives us, redeems us, and makes us His children, He shows us His wonderful love and His amazing grace. He shows His power, love, and compassion, even in the midst of terrible tragedies.

Moral evil, on the other hand, may be expressed through immorality, delinquency, dishonesty, lying, purposely misleading others, iniquity, committing murder, doing harm to another, using God's name in vain, stealing, hating others, not forgiving others, not paying our bills, refusing to love and help others in need, and many more sins.

As Christians, we believe in the reality of moral evil. However, liberals, some of whom claim to be Christians, deny the existence of evil. In their efforts to be politically correct, they are not comfortable with the thought of judgment on sin and evil. Even though some of them basically agree with it, they feel it is bigoted to talk about it. The Bible says, "For the wages of sin is death ..." (Rom. 6:23). Evil does exist, and we must be rescued from it.

How did moral evil come into this world? Satan (Lucifer) was an angel who rebelled against God and was kicked out of heaven. Jesus said, "I saw Satan fall like lightening from heaven" (Luke 10:18). Then, when Adam and Eve were living in the garden of Eden, Satan appeared in the form of a serpent. He tempted Eve to disobey God, and she ate the forbidden fruit. (See Gen. 3:1–7.) After she had eaten, she gave some fruit to her husband and he did eat. When this happened, they both realized they were naked and made themselves clothes out of fig leaves. They had now yielded to the Evil One, and sin (disobedience and evil) had now come into the world. They brought evil into this world, and it has been a problem for every generation since that time.

In many situations, lingering and even disabling illnesses are the result of moral evil. Not all illnesses, however, are the result of sin. In the gospel of John, Jesus was confronted by a blind man who had been blind from birth. His disciples automatically assumed his blindness was caused by sin. They said, "Rabbi, who sinned, this man or his parents, that he was born blind?" (John 9:2). "Neither this man nor his parents sinned," said Jesus, "but this happened so that the work of God might be displayed in his life" (John 9:3). In this instance, what appeared to be evil was not so. This man's blindness was for the purpose of declaring the glory of God. So we can't assume that every disabling condition or physical disaster is the result of evil.

Multitudes of people in every generation have suffered eternal death from evil. Satan is a master at hiding the dangers of evil. Satan can "masquerade as an angel of light" and deceive the very elect of Christ. (See 2 Cor. 11:14.) We are constantly in danger of being deceived by Satan. In the last petition of the Lord's Prayer, Jesus tells us we are to ask God to deliver us from the grasps of the Evil One. We must never allow ourselves to take on Satan alone—because he will defeat us. Only God has the power to go into battle with Satan and come out the victor. "Our Father ... deliver us from the evil one" (Matt. 6:9–13). Natural evil kills the body; moral evil brings eternal death to the soul.

All our hope for eternal life and security depends on the power of God to keep the promises He made to us. God has promised eternal life to each of us who have accepted Christ as our Savior. In the gospel of John, Jesus says, "My sheep listen to my voice; I know them, and they follow me. I give them eternal life, and they shall never perish; no one can snatch them out of my hand. My Father, who has given them to me, is greater than all; no one can snatch them out of my Father's hand. I and the Father are one" (John 10:27–30). This is our hope for eternal life; it is our only hope. Our hope for the rest of eternity can only be realized and actualized through Jesus Christ, our Lord and our Savior. We can trust Him with our soul; He has never failed His children.

God can help us overcome, manage, and recover from natural evil; He will give us strength, divine leadership, and ultimate spiritual victory over moral evil. We serve a God who can handle victoriously any situation that comes into our lives. He can, and will, meet our every need.

We close this study of the Lord's Prayer with these words: "Hallowed be thy name."

CONCLUSION:

"Model Prayer Menu"

W E NEED TO INTEGRATE the model prayer into our everyday life to help us understand what this prayer teaches. We must remember: the Lord's Prayer is a model for us to follow as we pray and as we live our daily lives.

Heavenly Switchboard: Hello, this is the Heavenly Switchboard. We are offering you a menu of services to help you expedite your requests concerning your life.

- If you are calling with an *untouched heart,* press "S" for salvation and turn to John 3:1–7, John 10:1–30, and Romans 10:9–13. Call your pastor or another Christian to help you be saved.
- If you are calling from a *touched but cold heart,* press "M" for mercy and get on your knees and pray for yourself. There is a chapter in this book for each need in this prayer.
  - ° If you need to give more attention to the general menu of services found in the model prayer, press 1.
  - ° If you are calling because you have profaned God's name inside or outside the church, press 2.

- If you are calling to inquire about getting into the kingdom of God, press 3.
- If you are calling because you are having trouble doing the will of God, press 4.
- You have just heard the menu for the primary section of this prayer. Once you have met the requirements of the first three petitions, you are eligible to make a request concerning the last four options of this prayer:
  - If you are calling about how to help pay your bills and feed your family, press 5.
  - If you are calling because you are having a problem forgiving people, press 6.
  - If you are calling because you are having a problem in dealing with temptation, press 7.
  - If you are having a problem getting out of the mess you have made with your life, press 8.

The Heavenly Switchboard is open twenty-four hours a day, seven days a week, fifty-two weeks a year for your assistance. Mercy, grace, and forgiveness are always available to meet your needs!

If you want this menu repeated, please turn to Matthew 6:9–15.

Structure of Model Prayer and Ten Commandments

Lord's Prayer

1. *Thy Name*

2. *Thy Kingdom*

3. *Thy Will*

4. *Us—Bread*

5. *Us—Debts*

6. *Us—Temptation*

7. *Us—Evil*

- 43 percent kingdom centered
- Start at the top and pray down
- Logical sequence

Ten Commandments

1. *No other God before me*

2. *Worship with no idol or graven image*

3. *Do not misuse the name of the Lord your God*

4. *Remember the Sabbath Day and keep it holy*

5. *Honor your Father and Mother*

6. *You shall not murder*

7. *You shall not commit adultery*

8. *You shall not steal*

9. *Do not give false witness against your neighbor*

10. *Do not covet anything*

- 45 percent God centered
- 55 percent human centered
- Obedience starts at the top

Top section (1–4): Requires us to have a right relationship with God.

"Honor your father and mother" (5): Transitional commandment between both sections.

Bottom section (6–10): Ethical—how we are to live with each other.

SELECTED BIBLIOGRAPHY

Barclay, W. 1958. *The Gospel of Matthew*, vol. I. In *The Daily Study Bible*, 2nd ed. Philadelphia: Westminister Press.

Bauer, Walter. Translated by William F. Arndt and F. Wilbur Gingrich. 1952. *A Greek-English Lexicon of the New Testament and Other Early Christian Literature (4th rev. and aug. ed.)*. Chicago: Univ. of Chicago.

Bruce, Alexander Balmain. 1956. *The Synoptic Gospels*. In *The Expositor's Greek Testament*, vol. I. Grand Rapids, MI: Wm. B. Eerdmans.

Evangelical Free Church of America. 1980. *Evangelical Beacon*, March 15. Chicago.

Harrison, Everett F., ed. 1960. *Baker's Dictionary of Theology*, 201-02. Grand Rapids, MI: Baker Book House.

Huddilston, J. H. 1950. *Essentials of New Testament Greek*. London: Macmillan.

International Bible Society. 1984. *The Holy Bible—New International Version*. Grand Rapids, MI: Zondervan.

Litt, Alfred Marshall D. 1960. *The Interlinear Greek-English New Testament*, 2nd ed. London: Samuel Bagster and Son.

MacArthur, John F. 1985. *Matthew 1–7*. In *The MacArthur New Testament Commentary*. Winona Lake, IN: BMH Books.

Strong, James. 2010. *The New Strong's Expanded and Exhaustive Concordance of the Bible.* Nashville: Thomas Nelson.

DURING THE GREAT DEPRESSION, people had to take any job they could get. Daddy took a job working on a farm just outside the city of Wichita Falls, Texas. The job provided an old farm house as part of the attendants' pay. My father, mother, older sister, and brother were living in that old, small house. But on December 9, 1933, the population of the house increased by two people.

In those days, most women had their babies at home, and that was where my twin sister and I were born. In 1933, most kids didn't know anything about having babies. My older sister was twelve years old and my brother was ten. When my mother was ready for our births, the doctor came to the house for the delivery. My sister and brother did not understand what was happening and were peeping around one of the doors of the bedroom.

Eva Lee peeped first and said, "Charles, Mama is having a baby!"

Charles said, "Let me see!" Then he peeped around the door, looked at Eva Lee and said, "You're not going to believe this, but there are two of them!"

I was the baby of the family by only ten minutes.

Mother must have given birth to us prematurely because we were both so small. My twin sister Betty weighed three pounds, and I weighed two and one-half pounds. Our first bed was a shoe box padded with light bedding.

When Betty and I were six months old, Mother and Daddy loaded all four children and our small amount of furniture on the bed of a T-model Ford, and we moved to Denison. We moved as a family, but Daddy and Mother got a divorce when Betty and I were about 13. Eva Lee and Charles had already moved out and were on their own.

My twin sister and I were raised in the poorest region of Denison, Texas: the Cotton Mill neighborhood. We had a one-parent home, and our precious mother provided for our needs. She worked hard; but God gave her the strength and health to hold up under the demands of her work. Mother brought home $32.50 a week, and the three of us lived on that amount of money.

My sister and I graduated from the Golden Rule Elementary School, which at that time consisted of eight grades.

After graduation we enrolled in Denison High School. I played football and ran on the track team. In 1949, I won district in the Mile Run.

At the end of the spring semester of tenth grade, I joined the Air Force and spent one year in service, receiving an honorable discharge.

In 1950, I went back to Denison High School and graduated in 1952, one year behind my sister.

By this time I had found Christ as my Savior and was saved. The Lord called me to the ministry, and I needed to go to college. I made arrangements to play football, run track, and play baseball in order to pay for tuition at the University of Corpus Christi.

After graduating from high school, I had married a Denison girl, Carol Joy Lee. Within a few months she was diagnosed with lupus erythematosis, which at that time had to be treated at the University of Texas Medical System in Galveston. I dropped out of school, and we moved to Houston.

During the time in Houston, I worked a secular job and enrolled part time at the University of Houston. My wife and I joined the Faith Memorial Baptist Church.

Within a year, the First Baptist Church in Needville called me to be their pastor, so we moved. It was in Needville that my wife passed away at age 21 and left me with two baby girls. Sheri was age 2 and Linda was 1.

Beyond my responsibilities of pastoring the Baptist church there, I had to give time and attention to my two girls. Their hair was pretty short then, and I kept their bangs trimmed in front. I would brush their hair on Sunday mornings and get them ready for Sunday school and church. I thought I did a pretty good job. However, when I arrived at church, some of the precious ladies would discreetly take the girls to the bathroom and fix their hair. They were afraid that I would be offended, but the opposite was true. I deeply appreciated their kindness and help.

The Lord worked with me, and I felt the need to go back to school to finish my education. After making several efforts to get back into a Baptist college, the Lord opened a door for me. This door led me to Marshall, Texas, where I enrolled in East Texas Baptist College. My mother asked me, "Billy, why don't you let me take those two babies and raise them for you."

I said, "Mama, I appreciate your willingness to help, but those are my babies, and I am going to raise them."

When I moved to Marshall, I had to find a place for my two little girls and me to live. There was one side of a duplex available that was in my price range, and it was reasonably nice, so I rented it. It had an extra bedroom, so I talked to some of the students at the college about subleasing the room to help pay the bills. A guy named Moody agreed to rent the room. Moody could have qualified as an old maid 90 to 95 years of age.

I had an automatic washer and dryer, so that saved me from having a laundry bill. One day I decided to wash some clothes. I had never used the washing machine before. After putting all the clothes in the washing machine (without sorting the colors from the whites, of course), I picked up a giant box of Tide and said, "Moody, about how much soap should I put in the washing machine?"

He thought a minute and said, "Man, I don't know. I've never washed clothes before."

I asked, "Do you think about half the box will be enough?"

He said, "You can start with that, and if it is not enough, you can always put in some more."

So I put in half the box of Tide, turned on the washing machine, and went down the hall to do something else. I started hearing a thumping sound, but I ignored it for a while. Finally I became concerned enough that I went back to the kitchen where the washing machine was, and suds were pouring out the top of the washing machine—the entire kitchen was about four to five inches deep in suds! I got a broom and started sweeping suds out the back door, while Moody was trying to mop them up. We had a lesson in housekeeping that day.

Another time, Moody and I were cooking a meal for ourselves and my two little girls. We decided to have some good country milk gravy like my mother used to make. We got into a discussion about what ingredients were to be used. I said, "Moody, I know my mother used some bacon grease, I think some baking powder, and I know she used flour and milk."

He said, "That sounds about right to me."

Then I asked him, "About how much flour do you think I should use?"

He answered, "Man, I don't have the least idea."

I said, "I guess we could start with a heaping cup, and if that is not enough, we can always add more."

We started thinning gravy, and thinned some more, and kept on thinning. We thinned gravy until every pan we had was full. That day, we received a good lesson in cooking. (As a side note, the girls did well—they never once went hungry.)

The Lord blessed me with an insurance job that provided sustenance for me and my two baby girls while I was in college. I serviced an insurance route in Marshall and Longview in Texas. The majority of the work could be done from about one o'clock in the afternoon to around nine o'clock in the evening. This allowed me to go to classes and get my lessons in the mornings and work Monday through Friday in the afternoons and evenings each week. Moody had been helping me with the girls, but he had dropped out of school and left town. I had to hire a babysitter. For some reason (I can't remember why), I came home early one night and found that my babysitter had my girls locked in a dark closet. I was furious. That was the closest I ever came to hitting a woman! I fired her on the spot and told her to get out of my house and not come back. I had other childcare problems after that, but none as serious as locking my baby girls in a closet. I prayed to God and trusted in Him, and He took care of all my problems.

I worked in the insurance business for about two years before Hillcrest Baptist Church in Marshall called me to be their pastor.

I pastored that church and continued my education at East Texas Baptist until my graduation in May of 1960.

It was in Marshall that I met Dene Powell, my present wife, and it was there that my third child, Lauri (another girl), was born.

During the third year of my pastorate at Hillcrest, the First Baptist Church of Bloomberg, Texas, called me to be their pastor. All my pastorates were very productive, and I had opportunities to work with many wonderful people. The membership of the church in Bloomberg was also made up of special people. We pastored in Bloomberg for two and a half years. While there, I felt the need to go to a seminary, and the wonderful people there made provision for me to enroll in Southwestern Baptist Theological Seminary in Fort Worth. The seminary provided living quarters and required me to be there Tuesday through Thursday each week. This required me to double up on my pastoral duties to make up for the time I was gone. The Lord blessed our ministry at the First Baptist Church, and attendance increased about one third over its previous size. We were extremely happy in Bloomberg.

During my second year in seminary, College View Baptist Church in Denton, Texas, called me to be their pastor. The members of the church in Bloomberg were so wonderful; it really made the decision to move a hard one to make.

We finally made the decision to go to Denton, and God blessed our ministry there. We outgrew the old facilities and had to build a new auditorium. We also renovated the old facilities to provide more Sunday school space. It was during our time in Denton that our fourth child was born. The Lord finally had blessed me with a boy, and we named him Richard. In May of 1963, I graduated from the seminary.

After a wonderful pastorate at College View, another church,

West Side Baptist Church in Atlanta, Texas—near Bloomberg—called me to be their pastor. We had a very good two-and-one-half-year ministry while at Atlanta. I felt the need to get more education, and I enrolled in the master's degree program at East Texas State University in Commerce, Texas. This university already had a soft spot in my heart because it was their stadium in which I had won district for Denison in 1949 in the Mile Run. I started in the program by enrolling in a Monday night class in counseling that was taught in Atlanta. After that, I continued taking classes on Saturday mornings on the university campus. In 1967, after two and one-half years, I received my master of science degree in counseling.

While in Atlanta, the urge to serve in the military became stronger. This led me to join the US Army Reserves as a chaplain. With my one year of active duty—and even though we made several moves—I was able to complete twenty-two years of military service, retiring at the rank of Major on December 9, 1993.

While serving in the Army Reserve, I enrolled in the United States Army Command and General Staff College at Fort Leavenworth, Kansas. I spent the last two weeks of that course in military science in residence at Fort Leavenworth and then received my degree. It took five years from the time I enrolled in correspondence courses until I graduated in August 1973.

It was also while in Atlanta that I completed enough of my master of science degree that I was offered a position as a personal and vocational counselor with the Texas Education Agency in Houston, Texas. So we moved back to Houston, where my wife taught school and where I was assigned to M. D. Anderson Hospital as a vocational counselor.

I served on a rehabilitation team made up of dentists from the

University of Texas Dental School and medical doctors from M. D. Anderson Hospital to rehabilitate maxillofacial patients after they had been treated for cancer. Our objective was to provide them with needed prostheses and train them in a vocation that was compatible with their abilities and disabilities. Then we had the responsibility to find a suitable place of employment for them. We did not have a 100 percent success rate, but we did help a lot of people and restore hope for many families.

After a couple of years, I was promoted to the position of supervisor for a group of counselors. At this time the Texas Rehabilitation Commission had become an independent agency. Our agency and the Texas Department of Corrections entered into a contract to work together for the rehabilitation of inmates while they were still in prison. Our agency provided training equipment for each program (through grant monies) and vocational counseling to inmates, while the Department of Corrections provided office space, job training personnel in many vocational areas, and other services to make this program a success. This educational system was the basis for the establishment, by the Texas State Legislature, of Windham Independent School District within the Texas Department of Corrections. The name Department of Corrections has since been changed to Department of Criminal Justice. The Texas Rehabilitation Commission placed a vocational counselor and secretary on each of the Texas prison unit campuses. I was fortunate to be assigned as the supervising counselor over all the vocational counselors in the southern prison units. After a few years, I was reassigned and became the supervising counselor for vocational counselors in the northern prison units.

After a few more years, I grew tired of working in the prisons and asked for a "free world assignment." The Texas

Rehabilitation program was in the process of decentralization, and they reassigned me to be the supervising counselor over ten counselors and secretaries and work with other agencies in establishing a rehabilitation program in northeast Houston. My territory included the area east of I-45 and north of I-10 all the way out to the Harris County line. We rented a significant part of a shopping center at the intersection of Little York Road and Highway 59 for our central work area. This resulted in a successful rehabilitation program for handicapped people for several years.

Throughout all these moves, changes in assignments, and new responsibilities, I pastored smaller churches and had no interruptions in my ministry for my Lord.

Once again, my wife and I became interested in making another change in our lives. Her parents lived in Oletha, Texas, and were both advancing in years. We knew they were going to need us, so we decided we would move to Central Texas to be near them. We sold our house in Houston and made other preparations to make the transition. Central Baptist Church in Thornton, Texas, called me as pastor, and the Lord also provided me with a secular job. I had been a bivocational pastor for many years at this point in my life. The Lord blessed me with a medical administrator job. The board of directors of Limestone Medical Center in Groesbeck, Texas, hired me to be the administrator. The clinic became successful to the point that we no longer qualified for the federal grant that funded it.

Then, I went back into the insurance business in Central Texas and became very successful.

After eight years, I felt the need to get back into an occupation that would utilize my training. I took a cut in pay to take a position at the Mexia State School as a behavioral therapist. I served in several other departments at the state school, and retired after serving more than two years as director of a workshop for handicapped people.

During my ministry in Thornton and tenure at Mexia State School, I also served three years as the Protestant chaplain at Providence Hospital in Waco, Texas. My working schedule had to be coordinated with my church and Mexia State School responsibilities. I would generally work two evenings a week and all day each Saturday. My responsibilities at Providence included patient visitations, assisting each time we had a crisis (such as responding to Code Blue), and preaching each Saturday at 4:00 p.m. on the hospital's television system that could be seen in all 234 rooms. This was one of the most fulfilling experiences of my life because there was so much ministering to hurting people. After three years my schedule proved to be too demanding, and I reluctantly resigned my position as the hospital's Protestant chaplain.

After serving as pastor of Central Baptist Church in Thornton for sixteen years, I was called to be the pastor of Victory Baptist Church in Groesbeck, Texas. As I write this book on the Lord's Prayer, I have been pastoring at Victory for nineteen years. We had wonderful people at Thornton, and we have wonderful people at Victory.

The Lord has blessed me with a number of fine grandchildren: Shawn, Michelle, Shelby, John, Shannon, R. C., and Shayla.

I hope the challenges, struggles, and blessings of my life and my family may speak to your heart and give you strength to trust our Lord on a daily basis.

After almost sixty years in the ministry, I am still learning the value of prayer in my life. My hope is that this study about prayer will be a blessing in your life.

In conclusion, please allow me to give an update on each person mentioned in this historical summary of my life. We will start with my mother, Eva Elizabeth (Jack) Anderson. She was born in November, 1898, in Texas, and passed away October 30, 1972, in Denton, Texas. What a wonderful mother she was. She shall always be loved and remembered. This earth was made a better place because of the seventy-four-plus years she lived on it.

My father's name was Lee Crawford Anderson. He was born August 5, 1893, in Texas, and passed away in Corpus Christi, Texas, August 11, 1968. My dad fought in the First World War in France and came back a broken man.

Please allow me to continue to give you an overview of all my family members, beginning with my oldest sister, Eva Lee Furche. Eva Lee was born December 4, 1921, in Texas, and passed away July 17, 2006. We buried her in the Oakwood Cemetery in Denison, where my mother is buried. Eva Lee had a son named David and a daughter whose name is Carolyn. David was a pilot in the Vietnam War and became a pilot with American Airlines after he became a civilian. David was born November 17, 1942, and died March 3, 2002, in Denton, Texas. Carolyn was born January 3, 1947, and lives with her husband, Ronnie Mitchell, near Howe, Texas. They have a daughter named Heather, who was born March 12, 1976, and lives in the Dallas area.

Next, we will share the story of my brother, whose life was filled with a mixture of blessings and heartaches. He and his wife, Melba Jean, had four daughters. When I was saved and called to preach, Charles, Melba, and their four daughters lived in the Cotton Mill neighborhood in Denison, Texas. I began sharing the blessings of my newly found faith with Charles, and he accepted Christ as his Savior. He joined Sunnyside Baptist Church in the Cotton Mill neighborhood, and his life was really turned around. He later received his call to preach and began pastoring churches. God blessed his ministry, and many lives were touched and changed through his and Melba's ministry. That is the blessing side of his life.

Now, let us consider his tremendous heartaches. One day, his youngest daughter, Eva Jo, who was a beautiful and sweet young lady of 18, began to have headaches. The situation worsened so quickly that medical attention could not reverse it, and one of her eyes just popped out of her head. She had developed a fast-growing malignant tumor on her brain. Within about two and one-half years, her life on earth ended in 1983.

Sometime later, their next youngest daughter developed a malignant condition in her hand. Her thumb was amputated, but the malignancy had spread throughout her body, and within about two years of the diagnosis, she died in 1995.

Then, their oldest daughter developed a severe diabetic condition that caused multiple internal problems, and she passed away in 1998.

This left them with one daughter, who was next to the oldest child in age. She began to have hip problems and was diagnosed with cancer. Charlotte had a natural musical talent that was God given. At five years of age, she could play the piano as well as the most gifted. She also was a great singer. We have had her come to sing at churches I have pastored, and the people left with tears in their eyes. She could have sung with the best gospel groups and brought them a blessing. They did surgery on her hip, but the cancer prevailed, and we had her funeral in 2008. My brother,

Charles, died in 2003, so he didn't live to witness the suffering and death of Charlotte, who was the darling of the family. She was not only the darling of the family, but she is also one of the darlings in heaven. I know she is using that beautiful voice and singing in the heavenly choir.

After Charles's death, this left the twins: my sister Betty and me. Betty contracted lung cancer, and her earthly life ended July 8, 2008. We buried her in Denton, Texas. She had lost her husband, Gene Hughes, a few years earlier.

After her death, that left only me out of all the children. I don't know why the Lord left me, the most unworthy of all the children. I used to look at Charles and Melba and wonder if I had the spiritual strength to endure what they had endured. At that time, I didn't know my time was coming.

When our oldest daughter Sheri was a senior in high school, she was diagnosed as having lupus erythematosis. Remember, her mother had died with lupus at the age of 21. This re-opened a chapter in my life that I had closed and put on a back shelf. Sheri's lupus progressed over the years, and she passed away in 2000 at age 46. She left a son, John, who is now grown and has taken a combination teaching-coaching job in Alaska.

My next older child was Linda. She married a fine man, Roger Pemberton, who is a successful executive with Hewlett-Packard in Dallas. Linda is a tremendous achiever, having completed her master's degree in nursing, and is very successful in her profession as a registered nurse. They have a son, Shawn, who has several strong abilities, though he also has a disability. He is very advanced in electronics, has a strong love for animals, and has started a pet supply business on the Internet. Shawn is a fine young man who loves to help other people, especially the disabled.

My third child's name is Lauri Jane. She is also an achiever. After finishing college, she worked her way through law school and is now a practicing attorney in Houston. She married a fine man named Thomas Taylor, who is self-employed as an independent home repair specialist.

My youngest child, my only boy, Richard, lives near us and is involved with cattle, horses, and some goats. Richard also has several rental houses—which keeps him busy. His wife, Tracy, is a teacher's aide in the local school district. They have four children at home ranging from a fifth grader to a senior in high school. Shelby is a senior, Shannon is a sophomore, R.C. is in the eighth grade, and Shayla is in the fifth grade. Richard has an older daughter, Michelle, who has a child with autism. Michelle is a wonderful mother who cares for her son, Donavyn, and is working on a nursing degree at the same time.

Looking back over our lives shows us how hard life can be. There is nothing more relevant to our needs than to be able to come to the Lord in prayer. I hope and pray that this book has been a blessing to you and taught all of us about our need for prayer to our almighty God and our Savior Jesus Christ.